GAMES MAKE SPELLING FUN

ACTIVITIES FOR BETTER SPELLING
Revised Edition

JOHN F. DEAN, Ed. D.
Chairman, Department of Education
Whittier College, California

Fearon Teacher Aids
a division of
Pitman Learning, Inc.
Belmont, California

The author wishes to thank Maude L. Frandsen for "Find It" and "Do You Know Me?," and Dorothea Martin for "Christmas Spelling Trees." Additional thanks go to William Conklin for "Advanced Football," Corrine W. Brown for "Speedy," and Mary Peavey and Nell Stillwagon for "Don't Say Unkle."

Printed in the United States of America.

ISBN-0-8224-3255-2

FOREWORD TO THE REVISED EDITION

Since its original edition in 1956, *Games Make Spelling Fun* has been used in classrooms with literally hundreds of thousands of elementary and secondary school pupils. Thousands of copies have been purchased for use with remedial high school students and adults, in the Peace Corps overseas, and in classrooms just like yours. The games have provided enrichment for brighter students, motivation for the academically disenchanted, and change-of-pace fun when the going gets tough.

As the title states, this little book is designed to help make spelling fun for your students. Not only is rote memorization anything but fun; it is rarely an adequate substitute for effective learning. *Games Make Spelling Fun* is essentially an idea booklet which can help you to teach spelling effectively. The games presented here will give your pupils extensive oral and written facility with their language, and they will supplement any good spelling curriculum. The new materials prepared for this revised edition represent a continuing effort both to improve the teaching of spelling and, as a secondary goal, to effect changes in the communication arts.

One word of caution: Don't tell your pupils that spelling is easy. If it is not easy for them, you could be creating two problems where there was only one. Admonished that spelling is easy, the youngster who is not finding it easy to spell correctly begins to feel incapable: if it is supposed to be easy and he still cannot do it, deductive reasoning tells him that he must be dull. These games, which give even slower children the experience of success, help to build up the expectation of success. And we all know that success tends to build success!

John F. Dean, Ed. D.
Whittier College

To get the most from GAMES MAKE SPELLING FUN

---

1. Build game standards with your class.

2. After each game, evaluate the results with your class

3. Plan to use one game each week. There are enough games to give a full year's enjoyment.

4. Save your duplicating masters. They will help you to remember that clever idea you used last year.

TABLE OF CONTENTS

CLASS ACTIVITIES

QUIET ACTIVITIES

CLASS ACTIVITIES

HOW TO USE THEM

The activities in this section are designed for the teaching of spelling through oral response, offering a medium by which a pupil may test his or her ability to spell or use a word orally. These activities will also help to overcome the stage fright present in many children, and will assist in achieving a social unity within the class.

All intelligent activity requires a critical evaluation. If you will take the time to conduct a careful evaluation of the games with your students, so that they can see what they have learned in a particular game, and what progress they have made, you will ensure the success and enjoyment of future games, and engage your students' interest and cooperation.

Of equal importance is your own professional review of the activity undertaken. Such an evaluation enables you to ascertain the true worth of any particular game to your class situation.

It is recommended that you become completely familiar with each game before you attempt it. The success or failure of each venture rests on the confidence your students place in the game.

TOP SPELLER OF THE WEEK

Recognition of pupils' achievement is strong motivation. Too often only the outstanding pupils can gain that recognition from the teacher or their peers. Try this method; it affords an opportunity to honor even the lowest achieving child. "Top Speller" is a confidence builder.

Construct the usual wall chart from a 24″ x 36″ tagboard. List the childrens' names down the left edge at half-inch intervals. Draw 37 vertical lines one half inch apart to provide one space for each week for each child. Number the columns for each week.

Present the ground rules, indicating that the title of "Top Speller of the Week" does not necessarily fall to the best spelling pupil in the room. The major criterion is effort and attendance to the task.

Friday afternoon is an appropriate time for the announcement. You can make the presentation more impressive by citing several examples of the criteria used in the selection for the week, and, with a flourish, placing the star or other indicator in the appropriate column by the pupil's name. The advantage of this recognition technique is that every child, regardless of his or her capabilities, has a chance of winning.

NAME'S THE GAME

The sweetest sounds in the world, particularly to children, are their own names. Teaching the proper spelling of each child's given name is a legitimate and well-received activity.

Select five or six names each week by any sampling device, present them as you would any new word, comment on similar letter-patterns found in other words they know, etc., and within a few weeks everyone should know and be able to write correctly the names of all the students in the class.

NAMES AND SAMES

Once the students have learned to spell the names of all members of the class, use the current spelling list to find similar sounds or letter patterns rhyming with the names of one or more students. The hazard inherent in this activity is finding similar sounds with differing spellings, and this may confuse the younger spellers. Be careful not to overemphasize the similar sound with differing spelling.

The primary goal in this game is to teach awareness of language sounds. The secondary goal is to clarify the phoneme-grapheme relationship.

QUIZ PROGRAM

Achieve a television show atmosphere by the use of a public address system, live or simulated. Once this is established, the children or the teacher may choose a child to act as the Master of Ceremonies. It's a good idea for you to be the first MC to show the children how it is done. After the initial experience, many boys and girls will be eager to attempt it.

The Master of Ceremonies calls on one of the boys or girls and says, for example, "Bill, one of the words in our list means 'to put'. Can you spell it for five points?"

Bill answers, "Place. *P L A C E*."

M. C. says, "That's fine."

Bill records his own score at his desk, and winners may be judged by the total number of points.

The points may be varied according to the size or difficulty of the word attempted.

WORD-O

Each child will divide his paper (8½" x 11") into sixteen equal parts by folding it. Into each space, on one side, he will write carefully one new word from the current spelling lesson, making a total of sixteen words.

The leader, probably the teacher, collects the papers and redistributes them throughout the room.

The leader calls out the words from the list and the children cover each word on the paper as it is called with discs of cardboard. The first child to cover a line down or across, or a diagonal line, as in bingo, is the winner.

As soon as the first child has completed the game, the papers are redistributed, ready to begin another game.

DETECTIVE

Write a word on the board from the current spelling lesson, leaving out one or more of the letters, depending on the level of the group. Give a definition of the word and call on individuals to fill in the missing letters. This may be done orally or in writing.

As the class matures, leave out more of the strategic letters and cut down on the definition clues.

By giving one point for each correct word, and allowing the children to keep their own scores, you will give everyone more incentive to study the words before the game is played.

FOLLOW ME

Choose a new or review word from the current spelling lesson to begin the game. State the word, then call on a pupil, who is supposed to give the first letter. The pupil then calls on another child to supply the second letter. This continues until the word is finished.

You may wish to have a recorder, a child who stands at the chalkboard and writes each letter of the word as it is spelled.

MATCH ME

This game requires two pupils of approximately equal ability who face each other and read the list of spelling words to each other, one at a time, as quickly as possible. The words must be pronounced correctly, and a record is kept of the time taken for the list. The winner is the pupil with the fastest time for a total of five attempts.

"Match Me" involves several learning activities. Small group involvement keeps pupils attending to the task; they see and hear the word at the same time, more than doubling the exposure; the words tend to become sight words, increasing the recognition speed of the word in context.

BASEBALL GAME

Divide the room into two equal teams.

Stake out a baseball diamond on the floor, indicating the bases with chairs or piles of books, or anything at hand that can be used as a marker.

Two of the better spelling students can be chosen as pitchers, to give the words to the opposing team.

The pitcher gives the opposing team three words — one each to the first three batters. If the first batter spells the word correctly, he is given a "single," and he moves to first base. If he misses the spelling, he is out.

If, before he is given the word, the batter specifies "Home Run," his correct spelling will clear the bases and that number of runs will be given to his team. In the event he misses the word, it is automatically three outs and the side is retired. Three outs must be registered before the opposing team takes the field.

WORD PICTURES

To begin the game, describe a word from the current spelling lesson according to its structure. The word *like*, for example, might be described as "a one-syllable word beginning with a consonant letter and ending with a vowel-consonant-*e* pattern." The word *best* might be described as "a one-syllable word beginning with a consonant and ending with a consonant blend."

Call on a child to find the word. When she does, she in turn will describe a word and call on a classmate to answer her question. The game continues until the list is completed.

HANGMEN

Two teams play this game. Each team chooses a leader.

On the chalkboard draw two sets of gallows. Under each gallows draw several lines of short blanks, each of which will be filled with a letter.

The first team selects a secret word from the spelling list. Their leader announces the number of letters in the word, and also marks off the required number of blanks with two vertical lines. He then calls on a member of the other team to give a letter that might be in the word. If the letter is correct, the leader writes it in its proper space; if the same letter appears twice in the word, it goes into both spaces.

If the letter called is not in the word, a head is drawn in the noose of the gallows representing that team, and the winning team takes its turn to guess. With each miss, additional parts of the body are added, and when the entire man has been drawn, he is considered officially hung. The team whose man is hung first loses.

It's wise to establish the body parts that will constitute the entire man before the game begins. Otherwise, the game might go on forever with the addition of more and more parts.

I'M THINKING OF A FRIEND

To introduce the spelling period, or during the few minutes just before lunch or dismissal for the day, try this one.

Begin by saying, "I'm thinking of a friend in the room whose given name begins with a consonant-vowel-consonant-consonant pattern. Can someone tell me who this friend is?" There may be several children whose names fit the pattern, but you would be expected to have one name in mind.

The pupil, when called upon, might say, "Is it Nancy? *N A N C* are the letters." You would respond, "No, it isn't Nancy, but the combination is correct. Very fine. Can anyone discover my consonant-vowel-consonant-consonant friend?"

Another pupil asks, "Is it Catherine? The letters are *C A T H*."

"Yes, it is Catherine, and the letters are *C A T H*. Congratulations."

This game serves several purposes. It is a continual reminder of vowel and consonant identification, and the teacher-student rapport is strengthened.

ELEMENTARY FOOTBALL

This game is played by two teams.

On the chalkboard, draw a football field to scale: 100 yards long divided into ten-yard segments. Put a circle representing the ball on the 50-yard line.

Each team is given six plays, represented by six spelling words, to advance the ball toward the opponents' goal line. With each word correctly spelled the ball advances ten yards. For each word missed, the offensive team loses ten yards.

Teams score six points each time they cross the opponents' goal line.

ADVANCED FOOTBALL

Two teams play this game.

The ball is put in play on the twenty-yard line of a football field drawn on the board. The offensive team is given four downs to advance the ball.

Each time, before a word is given to a team member, he must choose either to run, punt, or pass. If he chooses to run, and spells the word correctly, the ball advances five yards. If he chooses to pass or punt, he may state the number of yards he wishes to go. If he spells the word correctly, the ball advances that distance. If he misspells the word, the opposing team may intercept the pass merely by spelling the word correctly.

In the case of a punt, usually on fourth down, a correct word will give the opposing team the ball at the point first chosen by the player in his yardage choice. If both teams misspell the word, the ball is returned to the line of scrimmage, or the point where the play began.

A fumble occurs when a player repeats the spelling of the word he is attempting. The ball may be recovered by the opposing team at that point if they spell the word correctly.

Ten yards must be gained by the offensive team in each group of four plays, or the ball is given to the opposing team.

Six points are given for each crossing of the goal. One point, the "conversion," is given for one more word spelled correctly after each goal is made.

IF TODAY IS TUESDAY . . .

Using the first letter of the name for that particular day of the week, spend a few minutes each morning reviewing all the words your pupils know that begin with that letter. With older children, the responses can be limited to certain categories. Sports, current events, teachers' names, cities and states, are all appropriate. Younger children will probably need an unlimited vocabulary from which to select.

For immediate reinforcement after the oral review, ask your pupils to write as many of the words as they can in a specified time limit, probably not exceeding three minutes.

Younger primary pupils who are not familiar with the digraph *th* may be allowed to use the letter *t* for both Tuesday and Thursday. When they are ready, the Thursday letter can become *th*.

"IN" WORDS

Supplement the weekly spelling list with "in" words, words which are enjoying a phase of unusual popularity. (For adults, these would be words like *charisma*, *serendipity*, *credibility*.) Words in current use, with their definitions, can be presented by you and the class on Monday. The words should be written on a chart, or on the chalkboard, or placed in the word boxes, or in any appropriate location.

Set a limit of five additional words for the week. If more are submitted, have the class select the five words for the week. Alert your pupils to read newspapers and listen to TV and radio discussion shows and news reports, as sources of "in" words. Politics, sports, fashions, music, and international events are all good generators of "in" language. Encourage all pupils to add the words to their spelling vocabularies, but test only those who wish to participate.

IS THAT REALLY A WORD?

Two or more teams can play this game.

The game is based on the fact that many words are built on a simple pattern in which a vowel-consonant ending is preceded by a single consonant or a consonant blend. Have an elementary dictionary on hand and appoint a good reader as referee. The dictionary is the final authority; also, no proper names are accepted.

Write *at* on the board. Explain to the teams that they are to take turns making words from the *at* pattern by adding a beginning consonant. They must follow alphabetical order, but they are to skip letters that will not make words. If a child gives a combination that doesn't seem to be a word, anyone on the other team can challenge, saying, "Is that really a word?" If the referee determines that it is not a word, the challenging team gains five points; if it is indeed a word, the challenged team gains five points. A challenge for not following alphabetical order is also possible, for two points.

Several patterns should be put into play before the game is ended in order to equalize the chances for challenge. Patterns include *in*, *it*, *en*, *og*, *all*, *ack*, *ot*, *ug*. Encourage your pupils to think of others.

Here's how the game might work: Begin by saying, "I went to the dictionary and I found *at*. Team One, what did you find?"

Team One's first member says, "I went to the dictionary and I found *bat*." Team Two's first member follows with *cat*. If the next person on Team One comes back with *dat*, Team Two can challenge by asking, "Is that really a word?"

If a chance to make a challenge is overlooked, you can challenge, but in that case no points are scored or lost.

To make the game harder for intermediate groups, have the teams work only with consonant blends, or with blends and digraphs.

Using both blends and digraphs, you would, for instance, get these words from *at*: *brat, chat, drat, flat, gnat, plat, slat, spat, that, what.*

Again, it is recommended that, as soon as the game is over, the children write as many words as they can in the patterns used in the game. This is a powerful reinforcement for spelling.

This game provides experience with spelling patterns. It also exercises dictionary skills, including alphabetizing, and involves the children in comprehending language structure.

WE DOUBT IT

Two teams play this game.

One child puts a letter on the board. An opposing player adds a letter, but he must have a word in mind. The object is to add a letter without finishing the word. (Two-letter words don't count.) When a player adds a letter that finishes the word, the opposing team gains a point.

If a player adds a letter and the opposing team feel he doesn't have a word in mind, they may say, "We doubt it." If the player can produce a word, his team gets a point; if he can't, the opposing team gets a point.

SPELL-OUT

Occasionally spell out the directions that the class is to follow. Have the children take down the words and then follow the written directions, but don't pronounce the words yourself.

Upper grades might enjoy being given the letters in a run-together form, and having to divide them into words first before they follow the directions.

FIND IT

Each child has a copy of the current words list, a pencil, and a sheet of paper. Begin by giving a definition of a word from the list. The children are supposed to find the word and write it on their papers. After each word has been written, pick a child to write the word on the board. The others check their answers against the board.

As the group progresses, the children may enjoy giving the definitions themselves.

DEAD OR ALIVE?

Have each child make a vertical fold on a sheet of paper. In the left column, the children are to list all the words from the current spelling lesson that refer to living things. In the right-hand column they write all the other words.

For variation, the children may be told to list words that show taste or smell, or words that indicate people, or words that indicate things that can fly or crawl, etc.

This activity tests comprehension and the ability to classify, and affords additional practice in writing the words.

DO YOU KNOW ME?

A pupil stands and spells a word from the word list without pronouncing it. She then calls on a friend to pronounce the word. If the friend fails to pronounce the word correctly, the pupil then calls on another person. The one pronouncing the word correctly becomes the next questioner.

HOLIDAY FUN

To add motivation to the spelling program, plan a bulletin board display in which the children may participate. In November, for example, a large turkey eating kernels of corn may adorn the room. On small pieces of yellow paper, shaped like corn kernels, print the names of the children achieving perfect papers on spelling tests. When the display is first made, no kernels are visible. As the month progresses, names are added to complete the display.

During the month of May, a May basket filled with paper flowers on which the names of the children achieving perfect papers are printed makes a decorative scene.

PANTOMIME

Two teams are needed to play this game.

Have each team, in its turn, choose one of the spelling words and act it out. Allow a three-minute huddle to plan the action, which is to be done without speech. If the other team guesses correctly, it scores one point.

If competition is not desired, have one child act out the word. The child guessing correctly becomes the next pantomimist.

NO-OUTS

Two teams play this game.

No-outs takes the form of the old-fashioned spelling bee, but does not exclude anyone. Points are given to the team spelling the word correctly. Whenever a child misses a word, he moves to the end of his line and continues to spell as his turn comes to him. The poor spellers thus receive as much practice as the outstanding spellers.

GRAB BAG

Write each spelling word on the board three times. Two of the spellings are incorrect. The children are to choose the correct spelling either by writing their choice on paper or by oral response.

Occasionally, insert a completely ridiculous letter, for the fun and added stimulation that will result.

If your group has a number of children who are poor spellers, it might be wise to make many of the choices quite apparent, so that these children also can achieve a degree of success.

COMBOS

Two teams play this game.

The teacher or leader will give a combination of two letters to the opposing team, and asks the members of that team to find a word in the current lesson using that combination of letters.

If the word given is correct, one point is given to the team answering correctly. If more than one word is applicable and is given, one point is scored for each additional word.

The teams alternate the questioning after each point or group of points.

CHRISTMAS SPELLING TREES

About the first of December, have the children cut small Christmas trees out of green construction paper. To each child who spells his words correctly on any day, give a small gold star. As any spelling task is performed correctly, add other colorful stars to his tree. Adjust the spelling situations to suit individual differences so that all children in the group will qualify for some stars.

The boys and girls can then make these trees into Christmas cards for their parents. The cards are well received.

THE TOPIC OF THE DAY

Divide the class into five equal teams for this game. Each team will have its turn once a week. Each team picks a leader and the team is called by his name.

Bill's team has Monday. His team's challenge is to name the topic for the day. After a huddle with his team, he presents the topic. Each team meets to write, in perhaps three minutes, all of the words it can think of that could be classified under that topic. If the topic is "Dogs," some of the words could be: *collars, fleas, fur, barks, toes, heads, legs, eyes, cats, trees, chases, poodle.* Correct spelling is not as important as the number of words, and the imagination of the students in making associations. The team leaders read the words aloud, and all of the different words are listed on the chalkboard, where they remain for the day.

The major objective of the game is to create word awareness. The increased vocabulary, the satisfaction, and the competitive spirit engendered are additional dividends.

CRYSTAL BALL

Try this for a quick review of the spelling list after the words have been introduced.

Select a word from the list. Write it on a slip of paper, fold it, and give it to one of the children for safekeeping. Ask the children to look into the "Crystal Ball," which sees all and knows all, and find the word you have written on the paper. Those who think they have found it are to raise their hands. When called on, the child says, for example, "Is it *dog*? D O G, *dog*?" If this is not the correct word, the teacher answers, "No, it is not *dog*, D O G, *dog*." If it is correct, have the child with the slip of paper unfold it and confirm that this was the word.

As children become acquainted with the game, they can take the role of leader.

SPELLING TAG

One child is chosen to give the first word. He walks around the room to tag a child to spell the word which he then gives to him. If the tagged child cannot spell it, the questioner continues looking for someone who can spell the word correctly.

The child giving the correct spelling then takes the first one's place and the game goes on.

PHONEME PHUN

Training the ear to hear sounds is an important objective of the language arts program. One successful method is to begin by saying, "Who can give me two words that begin with the sound (e.g.) /ch/ as in *chest*?" The pupil replies by giving two words which he believes satisfy the request, and then spells the beginning sound. You may then ask others in the class to tell the words they had in mind. This can be done orally or in writing. You may prefer to have the pupil supplying the correct answer become the next questioner.

The game could be based on past spelling lessons, so that the pupils can scan them when they cannot recall particular words. However, it is better not to restrict pupils' reponses to the spelling lists, but rather to encourage them to think of any word in their vocabulary. Either way, the phoneme-grapheme relationship is reinforced, and the child gains experience in learning how to approach the spelling of "unknown" words.

WORD BOWLING

To prepare for this game, make a duplicator master consisting of ten rectangles, 1″ X 2″, arranged in the pyramid shape of bowling pins ready to be played — successive rows of four, three, two, and one. Distribute the sheets and have your pupils write or print one of the spelling words from the current list in each of the ten rectangles, following any order.

Choose one child to be "bowler." The bowler calls out a word from the list. If the word appears on a child's sheet, the child places an *X* through it. Ten words are called. Those with the fewest words crossed out are declared the winners.

The major benefits of this game are in the writing, verbalization, and high level of interest and attention.

WHICH WORD?

After the weekly spelling test papers have been collected, ask questions such as the following about words on the spelling list. Children who think they know the answer to a question raise their hands. Choose one or two to write the answer on the board. If the level of the class permits, children should be required to answer without referring to the spelling list.

Write any word from our list which has in it the sound /shun/.
Write a word which has three vowel letters.
Write a word which has two (three) syllables.
Write a word which begins with a consonant blend.
Write a word which contains a double consonant.
Write the word which comes second in alphabetical order.
Write a word that ends with the vowel-consonant-*e* pattern.
Write a word that shows a plural form.

Since the answers are being written on the board, they can be discussed at once, providing immediate positive reinforcement. This activity, which tests recall and heightens children's awareness of word structure, can easily be modified to use as a written exercise.

QUIET ACTIVITIES

HOW TO USE THEM

These activities are designed for the teaching of spelling through written response. They will also aid you in locating writing problems, and will test individual children's ability to follow directions. In addition, many children who do not excel in oral situations for any number of reasons may gain recognition by fine examples of written work.

Various techniques have been incorporated in this section by virtue of which children may be expected to show spelling growth. Some of these are:

1. Repetition. Stimulated repetition far exceeds all rote methods for real learning.
2. Emphasis on meaning. A link between spelling and meaning is present in many of the games, giving the child opportunities to use the new words.
3. Attention to configuration and structure. Research shows that both of these concepts aid in spelling.
4. Reinforcement. Class reviews and discussion, writing on the board, and recognition for children achieving at all levels, are included in many of the activities.
5. Creative activities. Children are encouraged to make use of what they learn in their own way through drawings and stories.
6. Dictionary use. Dictionary skills are basic to learning how to spell.

The success of these quiet activities rests primarily upon successful presentation. Always make sure that each game is clearly understood before the children begin to work on their own.

CROSSWORD PUZZLE

Make up a fifteen-by-fifteen square crossword puzzle, using the new and review words in the current lesson. To make your task easier, don't try to use all the words; fill in with everyday words and some from the social studies unit. Make the definitions simple, and don't forget a little humor. Children like puzzles, and will learn definitions and spelling from them without considering it work!

Provide each child with a copy of the puzzle. If a duplicating process is not available, draw the puzzle on the board and have the children copy it.

CROSSWORDS

Make up a large supply of 8½" x 11" paper with half-inch squares.

Ask the children to make up their own crossword puzzles by crossing words from the current lesson, starting with one word across the center of the paper. You may need to start them off with the first cross. After one or two experiences, they should be able to start on their own.

```
 C
 R
WORDS
 S   P
 SUPPLY
     E
     A
     S
     U
     R
     E
```

Give special recognition to those who have been able to use every word in the lesson. This activity can be repeated with every weekly list.

A LETTER IN A LETTER

Cut out letters of the alphabet, in various sizes and type faces, from magazines and newspapers. Put each letter in a small envelope, except that the following letters should be doubled up: *I* and *J*, *K* and *L*, *Q* and *R*, *T* and *U*, *W* and *X*, and *Y* and *Z*. This gives you 20 different choices. There should be more than one of each kind, so make duplicates of some of the envelopes.

The envelopes are put in a large paper bag or other container and thoroughly mixed. Then each child picks one. The child's task is to search for and write down all the words in the current and three previous spelling lists which begin with the letter or letters in his envelope.

Well-written papers can be displayed on the bulletin board. Give special recognition to pupils finding the most words for a particular letter. Recall envelopes to use on other occasions.

As a variation on this game, the children can be directed to find their words on certain specified pages in their reading books.

OPPOSITES

From the spelling lists your pupils have already studied, make a list of words for which there are antonyms, and duplicate the list. The children are to write an "opposite" (antonym) for each word on the list. Afterwards, all the opposites that have been thought of for each word can be written on the chalkboard for all to see and discuss.

Keep dictionaries handy and encourage your pupils to use them for help in finding opposites and checking their spelling.

Older groups may be instructed to make their own lists by finding opposites for words in the last three weeks' spelling lists.

MAKE A LITTLE DICTIONARY

Have children put the weekly spelling words in alphabetical order. Depending on the grade level, they can then either draw pictures to illustrate some of the words, or they can write little definitions of each word. In the intermediate grades pupils can work with a greater number of words, using two lists of spelling words.

Once the words are in alphabetical order your pupils might like to put them in booklet form. Have them fold sheets of paper in half, stapling two or three together in the fold, and use these to write in the words and definitions, and perhaps draw some illustrations. These can be taken home, or exhibited on the bulletin board.

SPEEDY

Use an overhead projector with a tachistoscope as a stimulus. Start showing spelling words at slow speed recognition, approximately one second, and lead the children up to 1/100th of a second. They can accustom themselves to quicker word recognition by experiencing spelling words flashed quickly in this manner.

The children's interest will be stimulated if you will occasionally insert the picture of a person or an animal.

ASSOCIATIONS

Each word in any given spelling lesson will have something in common with another word on the list. That association may be found in common beginning or ending letters, in prefixes or suffixes, in similar vowel sounds (with or without similar spelling), or in merely the identical number of syllables or letters.

Have the children make as many word pairs as possible by looking for such associations. They should write these word pairs on a sheet of paper and be ready to discuss them. Give special recognition to the children finding the greatest number of associations, and the most interesting associations, within a given period of time.

NAME FUN

Each child is to choose and write on his paper the name of a town, state, or friend. Check to see that the name is spelled correctly. Now explain to your group that they are to write every word from their spelling list that uses one or more of the letters in the chosen name.

Individual recognition is a great stimulus for work of this type.

DON'T SAY UNKLE

A misspelled word is taken from the pupil's work. He and the teacher discover the difficult part of the word, and he attempts to find words with letter patterns similar to those in his misspelled word. For example, *quiet* and *diet* have an identical letter pattern. Prefixes like *pre* and suffixes like *ing* can also be handled as letter patterns.

Let each child take his misspelled words home, after discovering their difficult parts, and the search for letter patterns will become a treasure hunt for him. When he reports his findings the next day, he will have a much clearer picture of the words most difficult for him.

WORD DOMINOES

This is a good activity when your class is making the transition from manuscript to cursive writing.

Cut tagboard or heavy paper into 2" x 4" rectangles. Draw a line dividing each rectangle into two 2-inch squares. In each square write one of the spelling words from the current lesson. Each word must be used twice, once in manuscript writing, the other time in cursive. However, a word must never appear twice on the same card.

The object of the game is to match the cursive and manuscript versions of the same word. The child is given the entire group of cards to work with. She begins with one card, then finds the matching card, and puts them either end-to-end or at right angles, as in dominoes. The activity continues until all the cards have been used.

HOW MANY?

After any lesson, such as arithmetic or social studies, have the children take paper and list all the words they can think of that pertain to the subject matter of the lesson. Give special recognition to those who list the greatest number of words. Have children read their lists to the class, and have all unusual or interesting words written on the chalkboard.

Such an activity may make a stimulating preface to a creative writing assignment in which the pupils are to try to use some of these new, interesting words.

SHORT STORY

Ask the pupils to write a short story using every word in the spelling lesson at least once. Allow time for children to read their stories.

Some of the most interesting or funniest stories may be posted on the bulletin board.

TRAVEL

After a discussion of road signs that the children have seen either in town or on the highways, have them list, from the current lesson, or their readers, words which might be found on road signs. Allow about ten minutes for the children to make the search, then share the results. Have the child tell the sign he had in mind when he gives his word — they can be signs of his own making, too.

SCRAMBLE

On a duplicator master, list ten of the spelling words for the week, with the letters of each word scrambled. Add two words that do not appear on the current list, so that you have twelve words in all. Direct pupils to put each word in its proper order. Further, they are to indicate, by encircling them, the words which do not belong on the current list.

COMPOUND CLUES

From time to time, at least once a month, develop a duplicated sheet giving clues to, or definitions of, halves of compound words that have been studied as part of the basic spelling vocabulary or as supplementary words. For example:

> The first part of the word is a round green vegetable. The second part is a hard-shelled seed. ______ ______ (peanut)

As the children improve in deciphering clues, omit the information about which is the first, and which the second part of the compound word.

"Compound Clues" also makes an excellent duplicated sheet for the Interest Center.

WHAT'S MY RHYME?

After the weekly spelling list has been introduced and the children are familiar with the words, try this approach.

Duplicate the list of words in one column, triple-spaced, and give one copy to each child. Next to each word, the child is to write a word which rhymes with the given word. For those words with difficult rhyming counterparts, have the children write words with the same letter patterns, such as *watch-hatch.*

In primary grades, possible rhyming words from which a choice may be made may be placed on the chalkboard.

ALPHABET ANIMALS

This game is particularly good for intermediate grades when the children are able to use a dictionary.

Each pupil folds an 8½" x 11" sheet of paper in half lengthwise, then writes the first thirteen letters of the alphabet down the left side of the first half, and the last thirteen on the left side of the second half.

The object then is to write, for each letter of the alphabet, the name of an animal that begins with that letter. (Birds, fish, insects, etc. are included). Pupils should be encouraged to refer to a dictionary to check for spellings and names.

It is recommended that you review this activity by calling on pupils to name the animal they chose after you give the letter of the alphabet. Each child who names a new animal for a particular letter writes the name on the chalkboard. In this way the entire class can see the words and note how they are spelled. This game also enriches vocabulary.

CASSETTE-TEASE

A twenty-minute cassette tape is best for this activity.

The teacher records a twenty-minute lesson on a cassette tape for use by pupils at the Interest Center. The lesson could be the usual game type, with the teacher requesting unique responses. For example, the teacher could record, "Hi, we're going to play a game with our spelling words. Do you have your spelling book? If not, turn me off, get the book, and come back soon, then turn me on again. Ready? You can use the last three lessons. Write the words beginning with a /sh/ sound. I'll give you one minute. Hurry! There are three of them."

The remainder of the lesson is composed of similar searching questions. Incidentally, if the teacher gives the answers at the end of the tape, it saves his time and assists in building a trusting and helping rapport between teacher and pupil.

By utilizing the entire twenty-minute tape, you get a timed experience. Once you and your pupils become familiar with the cassette technique, each will find many other uses for this great medium.